W9-BFQ-172

Made to Grow

Robert and Annelle Harty

Illustrations by Bill Myers

BROADMAN PRESS NASHVILLE, TENNESSEE

© Copyright 1973 • **BROADMAN PRESS** • *All rights reserved* • 4242-22 • ISBN: 0-8054-4222-7 •
Dewey Decimal Classification: C612.6 • *Printed in the United States of America*

You may live in a large city or in a small town.

You may live in a medium-sized city or in the country.

You may live in a house, an apartment, a mobile home, or a duplex.

Wherever you are, look around you.

What do you see?

You may see a mother and a father or a grandmother and a grandfather.

You may see a brother or a sister or lots of them!

You may see people on the sidewalk or a neighbor next door.

You may see a pet—a dog, a cat, a turtle, rabbits, fish.

Everything you see had a beginning. Everything you see was made for growing. You, too, were made to grow.

God Planned for Growing

God planned for growing a world—
   . . . the heavens and the earth
   . . . light and darkness
   . . . water and land
   . . . grass and trees
   . . . water creatures and birds
   . . . cows and even lions
God commanded everything he had made
to grow and to multiply (make many).
"And God saw that it was good."
God planned for making a man.

Then God said, "Let us make man in our image."

The world will be his to use
. . . the fish
. . . the birds
. . . the cattle
. . . the earth
. . . the creeping things

God made Adam, the first man.
God breathed into him the breath of life.
Then man began living and growing.

God Planned for Growing a Family

"God said, 'It is not good that man should live alone.' "

God made Eve, the first woman. God created both male and female.

Adam and Eve became a family. They were different from the other living things.

God said to them, "Be fruitful and multiply."

Their family grew when Cain was born. The family grew larger when Abel was born.

Ideas About Growing

Are all living things alike?

Why are people of two sexes—male and female—boy and girl?

Are all living things born from mothers?

Where do living things come from?

All living things—plants, animals, and people—were made by God. Each living thing is alike in some ways and different in other ways.

small—large
tall—short
rough—smooth
fast—slow
male—female

Each living thing was made for a special reason. God planned for life to continue on the earth. Plants, animals, and people can pass life on and on for generations.

Each creature's babies are like itself so that each type of life may go on.

Birds are born from eggs laid by the mother bird.

Baby chickens are born from eggs laid by the mother hen.

Spiders, insects, and some animals are born from eggs.

Trees grow from seeds produced by the parent tree.

A baby begins when a male sperm joins with an egg inside a female. The egg then develops into a baby.

Both sexes—male and female—are important to begin a life.

Living things have a beginning and an end. They start life, they grow, they go on living, and they die. While they are living, they can produce other living things like themselves—they can reproduce. If living things did not reproduce, life would not continue on the earth.

Growing from Mother and Father

You may not know how your life began.

During all his work of creating, God made man and woman, male and female, so life could be passed on and on. Each sex, man and woman, is different from the other but equally important.

When a man and a woman love each other and want to become husband and wife, they get married. Marriage is pleasing to God.

It takes a man and a woman to start a baby. Both parents are important—both a mother and a father are important. Children need the love and care of both a father and a mother.

A baby is born either a boy or a girl—
male or female. Both boys and girls have
arms and legs, but their bodies have some
differences, too.

A boy has a body part called a penis,
located between his legs. Behind the penis
is a pair of testicles, hanging in a skin sac
(scrotum).

A girl has a body part called a vagina, an opening or passageway, located between her legs.

Besides the penis and vagina, sometimes called sex organs, there are other parts which help make babies.

Inside the woman's body there are ovaries which make and store egg cells. There is a uterus where the egg cell can grow into a baby.

The man's body makes sperm cells, and they are stored in the testicles.

The sperm cells go out of the father's body through the penis and into the mother's body through the vagina.

Life begins when a sperm cell from the father joins the egg inside the mother.

Your life began when a sperm cell from your father joined an egg inside your mother. This made you! Your life began when your father and mother expressed their love for each other in this physical way.

Growing into a Baby

You began as a tiny cell no bigger than a dot made with a pencil.

Every person you know began growing when a sperm cell and an egg joined each other . . .

mother	brother	friends
daddy	sister	teachers

Your skin may be white, or brown, or yellow, or black. You may live in America, or in India, or in Africa, or in China.

Every person everywhere began as a tiny cell.

What a miracle of God it is, that such a small thing can contain all that you have become—your fingers, your legs, your head, your whole self.

The baby grows and grows inside the mother's body in a place called the uterus.

Sometimes more than one egg is inside the mother's uterus. When sperm cells join the eggs, more than one baby grows inside the uterus . . .

twins—two babies

triplets—three babies

quadruplets—four babies

. . . all can grow at one time inside a mother's uterus.

The tiny cell that would become you grew larger and became many cells. As they grew, the shape of the cells changed. The shape of the mother's body also changed.

Three months. . . .

You kept growing month after month. Everything you needed to help you grow was provided in the uterus. Your mother's body furnished food, oxygen, warmth, and protection. A tube called the umbilical cord helped to provide a passage for food and oxygen from mother to baby. The cord grew out of your body where you can now feel and see your navel.

Five months. . . .
Soon you began to look more like a baby. You had tiny arms, legs, eyes, nose, ears. You began to move, helping your mother to know that you were alive.

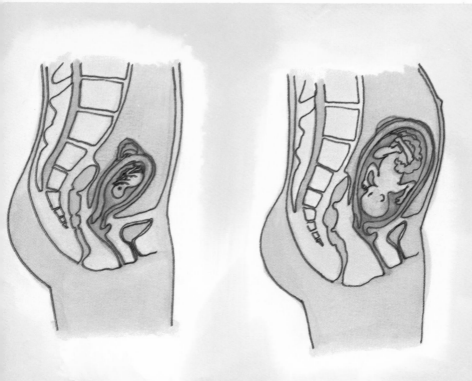

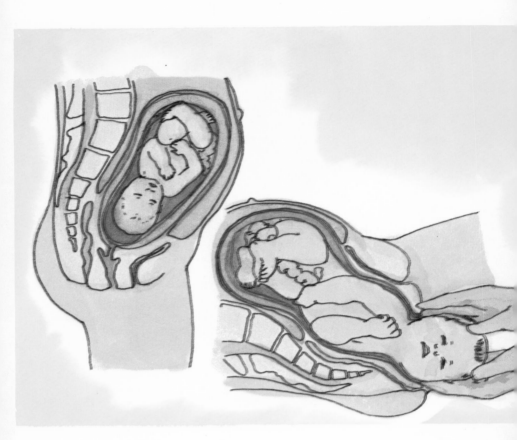

Seven months. . . .

Everyone in a family gets excited waiting for a new baby. Even the neighborhood gets excited. What will the baby look like? Will the baby be a boy or a girl?

Nine months. . . .

While people were getting ready for you, you were getting ready to be born. You were getting ready to leave your inside home to live outside of your mother's body.

You lived inside your mother for about nine months. That is the amount of time it takes a baby to grow enough to be born.

Finally you were ready to leave your mother's body. Your mother's body knew you were ready to be born. Your mother stretched and pushed, and out you came. You came out through an opening called the vagina.

Most babies in our country are born in a hospital. Doctors and nurses help the baby to be born and then help take care of both the mother and the baby.

After four or five days in the hospital the mother and baby can go home.

Now you know how you lived in your mother's body before you were born. You know how you grew from a tiny egg and sperm—a cell—into a baby.

Growing Together

When you were born you became a part of a family.

Families are different. Is your family small? It may be large! There may be brothers and sisters, a grandmother, aunts, cousins in your family.

A family is a place for belonging.

You help make your family a happy one.

Each person born is different, but each person takes on characteristics of his parents, his surroundings, and his experiences. We are more like members of our family than like other people.

Each family member is important.

The mother in a family is important.

She gives warmth, protection, comfort, and love to the newborn baby.
She cares for the physical needs of the family.
She sees that all have food and clothes.
She helps teach and guide the child in a family.

The father in a family is important.
Boys often want to be a man like their father.
Girls learn what men are like from their father.
The father usually works to earn money for food, clothes, and shelter for his family.
He helps to teach and guide his children.

A child is important in a family.

The child is a living, visible result of the marriage relationship.

The child is a person to love and one who gives love.

A child makes a family happy by talking, sharing, and helping.

Boys and girls are important—but different.

Each person is different from every other person. You are the only person just like you. No one else can be just like you. This is so because God thinks you are a very special person.

Each individual person in a family is important.

Families are for living, loving, and sharing. Families are for working, playing, and worshiping.

God's plan for families was a good idea.

Growing Up Is Good

When you were a newborn baby

. . . you had to be fed every few hours;

. . . you had to be kept clean, warm, and dry;

. . . you needed a lot of sleep to help you grow.

As you grew older

. . . you stayed awake more;

. . . you smiled and made noises;

. . . you ate more solid foods.

Later you learned

. . . to sit

. . . to crawl

. . . to walk

. . . to speak

Now you can

. . . dress yourself

. . . go to school

. . . have ideas and feelings

You are still growing and learning.

Growing Up Brings Changes

What does it mean to be a boy?

What does it mean to be a girl?

From your birth, your mother and father begin treating you as a boy or as a girl by what they said and did.

As you grow, you copy what others do.

Boys copy men. Boys become more interested in things that men do.

Girls copy women. Girls become more interested in things that women do.

We sometimes call things men usually do "masculine." Things women usually do are called "feminine." This is not always true.

Sometimes people get confused about what masculine and feminine mean.

A man can be gentle and tender like a woman. He can comfort small children. A man can write poetry, paint pictures, be a ballet dancer, and still be a man. He is still masculine.

A woman can be strong like a man. She can earn the family living. She can do repair work or mow the lawn. She may choose to be a doctor, to design bridges, to run races, and still she is a woman. She is feminine.

Boys and girls are different from the beginning of life.

A boy grows up to be a man. He can be the father of children.

A girl grows up to be a woman. She can have babies when she is old enough to marry and take care of them.

Growing up happens at home, at play, at church, and at school.

Growing up brings many changes in mind and body.

In God's plan, we are made to grow and to change.

One Sunday I selected from a display a tract on what the Bible says about sex. The word "sex" was printed in extremely large lettering. My nine-year-old son remarked, "Hey, Dad. You gonna read about sex?" As he said this he grinned and animated his eyebrows and face quite knowingly. This same remark and expression occurred several times. Feeling it was time to have a talk with him, I asked him to tell me what the word "sex" meant. First, he replied, "Nothing much."

I said, "I really want to know what you think."

"That hugging and kissing stuff," he replied.

Because children develop at different levels, we sometimes mistake their questions and reactions to mean far more than they really do.

It is not unusual for boys and girls to become interested and curious about what girl bodies and boy bodies are like. They wonder about the functions of certain parts of the body. It is a natural and healthy thing to be curious and to find out about things of interest.

If you have one or more children, or work and observe children, you quickly discover that every child is different and develops differently. This book is designed and written to help you

as a parent,

as a teacher,

as a grandparent,

as an interested observer

help children discover what growing up is all about.

As you guide your child in his growing experiences, you as a parent may want to

read this book to him the first time;

encourage your child to check the book from the library;

purchase a copy of the book to keep at home permanently for reading and referral.

Before your child reads this book, why not take a look at it yourself. It may help you to grow more adult.